From GLORY *To* SHAME

From GLORY *To* SHAME

The Rise & Fall of Black America And How She Can Rise Again

Samuel L. Madison

FROM GLORY TO SHAME: THE RISE AND FALL OF BLACK AMERICA (AND HOW SHE CAN RISE AGAIN)

Cover Design by Bill Hopper of Hopper Graphics

TORCH LEGACY PUBLICATIONS: DALLAS, TEXAS; ATLANTA, GEORGIA; BROOKLYN, NEW YORK

First Printing, 2007

The Bible quotations in this volume are from the King James Version of the Bible.

Printed in the USA.

ISBN: 0-9785333-2-1

"Character, not circumstances, makes the man."

–Booker T. Washington

DEDICATION

I dedicate this book to the members of my family for their unwavering and immense support. I am indeed grateful to my wife, Juanita Madison, who has stood with me through thick and thin, over the many years. Also, I owe a debt of gratitude to my three wonderful children: my son, Daryl; my twin daughters, Natosha, and Santosha; and to all people who are striving to bring Black America back from *SHAME to GLORY*.

From Glory to Shame

CONTENTS

ACKNOWLEDGEMENTS

This book would not be possible without the labor of love from the staff of Torch Legacy Publications. I want to especially thank: Daniel Whyte III, president of Torch Legacy Publications, for believing in this project; Daniella Whyte, my editor, for her hard work on this project; and, Bill Hopper for designing the beautiful cover. But most importantly, I want to thank God for allowing me the privilege to write these essays to hopefully help the Black community of America and whosoever will.

"Glory built on
selfish principles,
is shame and guilt."

–William Cowper

INTRODUCTION

by Samuel Madison

It is obvious from recent newspaper articles and news reports that many people are concerned about some of the painful problems in the black community of America. And we cannot deny these problems. The black community, in general, has some very serious issues. You know it, and I know it. None of us want to air our dirty laundry, but we must deal with the truth, because as Jesus Christ said, ***"The truth shall make you free."***

Thankfully, many African-Americans are doing quite well. We know that all blacks are not out there committing crimes such as we hear in the media daily, particularly in our urban areas. But unfortunately, many in our community are doing things that are not only hurting others, but are also hurting themselves, especially among our young people. Yes, these crimes are committed by other races as well, but that is no excuse for what we are doing.

Why are our young people murdering one another and others? Why are they left to themselves? Why isn't anyone taking responsibility? Why are we allowing the glory that we once enjoyed, to be stripped from us, and our present and future turned into shame? We have serious problems in our community, and it is going to take people who will stand up, acknowledge the problems, tell the truth regarding the problems, and offer solutions to change the terrible state of affairs in Black America.

In this book, ***From Glory to Shame***, I compare the problems in the Black community of America today with the problems the Israelites had in the day of the Prophet Hosea. I deal with the judgment that God brought down on the Israelites for their rebelliousness, "stiff-neckedness," and foolishness. Then I delineate the issues that we as Black Americans have today that stem from our own rebelliousness, "stiff-neckedness," and foolishness, and the judgement of God that is obviously coming down on our community. I not only discuss the social issues of the Black community, but I also share some insight about the religious and spiritual issues of Black America. Yes, indeed, Black America is religious, but, sad to say, we are not as Biblical as we should be. Lastly, I share Biblical solutions to help us as a race get out of the downward spiral, and start ascending back from "Shame to Glory."

I am very thankful for the great work that Tavis Smiley spear-headed resulting in the powerful new book entitled, ***The Covenant with Black America***. One of the things that I like about ***The Covenant with Black America*** is that after each chapter, it has a section dealing with *"What the Community Can Do,"* and then *"What Every Individual Can Do."* I really love that aspect of this great work because it says we are not just talking here, but we are about doing something.

Well, obviously, it was not the intent of ***The Covenant with Black America*** to deal with the spiritual aspect of turning Black America around. But I believe the spiritual aspect is the most important aspect if we are going to see great, positive changes in the Black community of America. And by the end of reading this book, you will know "What the Community Can Do" and "What Every Individual Can Do" to make Black America truly better from the inside out. "So start reading!"

—Samuel L. Madison
Atlanta, Georgia

"As they were increased,
so they sinned against me:
therefore will I change
their glory into shame."

–Hosea 4:7

Chapter 1
From Glory to Shame

* * * * * * *

One Sunday evening, while my family and I were anxiously awaiting the six o'clock news to see if those who were responsible for committing the triple murders at McFrugal Auto Rental in Atlanta, Georgia had been apprehended, my daughter asked me a rather stunning and perplexing question. Apparently, she had begun to notice that more than ever, I had become quite distraught over the depressing news of hearing about so many blacks being responsible for committing many of the heinous crimes taking place in and around metro-Atlanta.

A Perplexing Question

The question that she asked me is perhaps one which I believe weighs heavily upon the minds of many blacks today, when they think of the black-on-black crime, and other violent crimes committed by blacks. She asked me whether or not I was ashamed of the declining morals of blacks in America and the negative image being reflected upon the black race.

The truth of the matter is that we cannot deny the declining morals of blacks and the negative image that is being displayed of us today. Here are some facts:

- African Americans constitute 12% of the U.S. population, 13% of the drug using population, but an astonishing 74% of the people sent to prison for drug possession.
- Nationwide, one in three young black men is under the supervision of the criminal justice system. In many cities, half the young black men are under the control of the criminal justice system.
- By the time they reach the age of 35, nearly eight in ten black men can expect to have been arrested, making arrest one of the unifying experiences of the entire generation.
- Black males account for 63% of all crimes in the U.S.

The Quest to be Black and Proud Again

My daughter's question carried me back to the sixties and the early seventies, when blacks had vigorously protested the dehumanizing Jim Crow laws of the South, and had come together under the principle of non-violent resistance as a show of force to change the plight of blacks in America. Until this time, blacks had been a people who were thought of by others as being lazy, shiftless, having no positive image of themselves, ignorant and unorganized in their efforts to devote themselves to any worthy cause. But, by divine providence of God, we were sent a leader in the person of Dr. Martin Luther King, Jr., who not only challenged the Jim Crow laws of a racist society, but who also challenged blacks to change the perception and the negative image that had been ascribed to the black race.

The Philosophy of Love and Non-Violence

Through the Biblical philosophy of love and non-violence, blacks began to make significant strides in establishing themselves as a vibrant and productive people in the mainstream of our society. Thus, blacks became more determined than ever to put forth a concerted effort as a people to be good and upright in their conduct toward others, even when they were mistreated. We became a people who were "black and proud." We were a humble, yet a powerful people who had taken charge of our lives. We were not a reactionary people, meaning that, when evil was committed against us, we would not react with harsh and punitive damage toward others. We were determined to exercise strength and self-control, even when we were ill-treated or in a combative situation. We could take pride in the fact that as a black people, though small in number, we could still take an undaunting and courageous stand against the evil stronghold of racism and prejudice in our society.

Yes, we were a people who could rejoice and celebrate in the new found truth that we were "black and proud." Those were the "Glory days" for blacks in America. We were knocking down racial barriers that had denied us our place of prominence and dignity for centuries. We were a people who were writing our own history. We were a people relishing in our glory.

The Vanishing of our Glory Days

Perhaps, I have out-lived my time, or maybe I am just no longer in touch with the thinking of this present generation. Whatever the case, I find myself in nostalgia, and wishing for those "Glory days," when much of the news reported in those days pertaining to blacks were centered around outstanding accomplishments that blacks had achieved. It seemed that blacks had a different agenda in those days than what this generation of young blacks seem to have today.

Blacks in the News then were Inspiring

During those "Glory days," we blacks could not wait

to gather around our television sets to hear about another door that had been opened to us; some other accomplishment that had been ascertained by blacks, where we had tunneled our own way through, or some other opportunity given to us, whereby we had taken advantage of an unprecedented situation, superbly met the challenge, and displayed excellent performance. It was exciting news in those days to hear about the first black judge appointed to the Supreme Court, the first black representative elected to Congress, the first black to serve as mayor of a large, urban city, the first black appointed chief of police of a southern city, and the first black chosen as the Heisman Trophy winner, etc.

Some Blacks in the News Today Vex the Spirit

Yes, unlike the news of those days, the news which we hear today concerning our people is indeed vexing to the spirit, to say the least. Ironically, the events that headline the six o'clock news today are still centered around blacks, but this time, no longer a thing of glory, but of utter shame. Today, we hear about blacks committing senseless crimes involving robberies, murders, drug addictions, car jackings, gangs, rape and all kinds of ungodly behaviour.

Incidentally, I am quite aware that these deplorable acts are committed by people of all races, but I get no satisfaction from this kind of argument, because I know that blacks still rank at the top of the list. Besides, my concern here is not about other people, but for my people. Therefore, I am highly disturbed by any news that places blacks in a negative light. It does not take any one long to realize amidst all the violence and corruption that is taking place today in the black community, that the "glory days," for blacks, have been turned to shame.

From Glory to Shame

As I read through Biblical history, I am reminded of how a people's life and destiny can be changed from glory to shame. The prophet Hosea, prophesied this about his people, the Israelites, that God would bring judgment upon His own covenant people, because they turned away from respecting and obeying the laws of God. The judgment of God would fall upon that generation of the Israelites' children.

"My people are destroyed for lack of knowledge: because thou has rejected knowledge, I will also reject thee, that thou shalt be no priest to me: seeing thou hast forgotten the law of thy God, I will also forget thy children. As they were increased, so they sinned

against me: therefore will I change their glory to shame."

-Hosea 4:6-7

From Glory to Shame: A Fulfilled Prophecy in the Plight of Israel

As we further examine the Scriptures, we learn that God did as He said He would do. He brought a judgment of shame upon the children of that generation of Israelites. We can further learn more about God's judgment pronounced upon the posterity of the Israelites in Hosea 4:10: ***"For they shall eat, and not have enough: they shall commit whoredom, and shall not increase: because they have left off to take heed to the Lord."***

We will not do an in-depth study of how God's judgment was implemented and how it affected the posterity of that generation of Israelites. However, even today, we can still see how the nation of Israel has suffered various types of persecution, discrimination, abuse and all kinds of misfortunes by the hands of other nations. It is also a nation that is torn asunder with conflict and threats of war—a nation of people still without peace and tranquility. From glory to shame certainly seems to have been the destiny of Israel—God's covenant people.

From Glory to Shame in the Case of Black America

Today is the fourth day since the triple murders that took place at the McFrugal Auto Rental in Atlanta, Georgia. I suppose today or tomorrow they will lay Charlie Carter to rest. I did not get to know Mr. Carter, although we lived in the same community. However, what I have read about him in the *Atlanta Journal-Constitution*, and have seen on television has impressed me. He was a loving father and a dear husband. Also, he was said to be an outstanding citizen in the community. I am sure there were other wonderful compliments that were said about him, but none of them would suffice for the way he and so many others are being killed today by young black males who seem to think that it is in vogue to gun someone down. What a pity! What a shame!

As I think about how we, as a people, have gone from glory to shame, I cannot help but to think about those of us who are responsible for having produced this kind of climate today, where too many of our young black males have been brought up without a father in the home. Statistics show that 53.5% of African-American homes are headed by a single mother (U.S. Census Bureau). Too many of us fathers have left the rearing of our children to the mother and to the welfare system. We have not been in the home to provide essential character building traits in the lives of our children. We have not provided responsible leadership, healthy role models, respect for authority, a strong work ethic and a Godly conduct for them to follow.

This generation is a misguided generation, that has placed too much emphasis upon material things, and not on traditional and spiritual values. Yes, we have failed miserably in our responsibility to our children. Yet, the most neglected area in which we have failed this generation, is to instill within them a wholesome respect for obeying the laws and commandments of God. We have rejected and forgotten the laws of God and God is saying to this generation the same thing He said to the Israelites: ***"...I will also forget thy children. As they were increased, so they sinned against me: therefore will I change their glory into shame."*** (Hosea 4:6b-7).

The drama that we now see being played out in the lives of our children in terms of desperate wickedness, is what I believe to be a direct result of God's judgment upon a people who have flagrantly rejected a knowledge of God's Word. Our only hope of regaining our dignity as a people and reclaiming the glory that we once enjoyed, is for us to condemn the lawless acts of our young people and accept responsibility for the fate of black America and stop blaming our actions on the white society. God's Word is true: ***"For if we would judge ourselves, we should not be judged"*** (I Corinthians 11:31).

"Some go to church to see and be seen. Some go there to say they have been. Some go there to sleep and nod. But few go there to worship God."

–Selected

Chapter 2
Religious, Church-Going and on the Way to Hell

* * * * * * *

I wonder why it is today, we see more than ever before, more people packing our church pews, more people caught up with gospel singing, more people shouting 'hallelujah' and 'praise the Lord', and yet we see less and less of true Christian living being fleshed out in our lives. I marvel at the many churches in both the white and black communities that have three worship services on Sunday and they are all packed out with overflowing crowds. What is even more astounding is that we are now beginning to see that some of these same churches have a tremendous increase in attendance for the Wednesday night services.

A Hypocritical Life

You cannot help but wonder why there is such an influx of people, nowadays, who are so religious, and yet their lives show no signs of being committed Christians. It seems that despite all the religious services and activities that they go to and are involved in, that still these activities have no profound effect upon their lives. In other words, there is no difference in their lifestyle from the lifestyle of the ungodly sinners who have made no profession of faith in Christ, and who have no place in their lives for religious activities. There is absolutely no difference in the lifestyle of those who profess to be Christians, who arise early on Sunday morning, tuck their Bibles underneath their arms, and rush out to attend an early morning worship service, than from those who make no claim of being Christians who rise early on Sunday morning to mow their lawns, and wash their cars while consuming a six pack of beer.

Sad to say, many of those who are on their way to catch an early morning worship service have just emerged from a life of sin just as the ungodly sinner. It truly amazes me concerning the number of so-called Christians who are involved with living in "shacking-up" arrangements and seem to have no guilt or remorse about doing so. How can it be, that these same people can attend a worship service, and yet not be convicted of the ungodly life that they are living? My only answer to such an enigma is that the reason one can attend worship service Sunday after Sunday, and yet not be convicted about his or her sexual sin or any other sin, is because the pastor of the church which he or she attends must not be preaching convicting messages on sin and exhorting the saints to live a life of righteousness.

How Some Churches Pack Pews

I suppose that much of the reason why some churches can have three Sunday morning services and pack the pews is because of the kind of "gospel" that is being preached. True enough, many people attend churches where pastors placate their congregation with an ear-tickling gospel. This also accounts for the reason why many so-called Christians can play the lottery, smoke dope, steal you blind, practice homosexuality, and then come to church and speak in tongues, roll all over the floor, shout and run around the church, and really believe themselves to be model saints. Why? Simply because the full counsel of the gospel is not being preached wherever these people attend church. Therefore, there is no conviction in regards to living in sin.

The Bible warns us of those who will come in the latter days preaching an ear-tickling gospel.

"For the time will come when they will not endure sound doctrine; but after their own lusts shall they heap to themselves teachers, having itching ears; And they shall turn away their ears from the truth, and shall be turned unto fables." (II Timothy 4:3-4).

Three Reasons why People are Religious, Church-Going and still on their Way to Hell

As I further examined this matter of how people are oftentimes religious, yet not biblical, I can think of three reasons as to why this is so:

The first reason why so many people are religious, but are not biblical in their position, is because *many of them are just simply not truly born-again Christians.*

Many of the people who are packing our church pews for a Sunday morning worship service are going to church because it affords them a fashionable lifestyle, and not because they have a personal faith in the Lord Jesus Christ. These people have equated the act of being in church as synonymous to that of being a born-again Christian. It is in vogue today to become a member of some church and to participate in the religious activities and services of that fellowship such as singing in the gospel choirs, teaching a Sunday School class, becoming a member of the Usher Board, and all such practices they believe will provide them with a salvation of good works. Thusly, these people are indeed religious but they are not biblically saved, and therefore have not experienced a change in their spirit and mind. A person who has been truly saved will be changed and renewed in his way of thinking, and would eventually desire to live a life of godly conduct (II Corinthians 5:17).

The second reason why people are religious, but are not right with the Lord, is due to *a lack of biblical conviction in their lives.*

There are many people who have adopted a religious lifestyle based upon what others believe about traditional Christian practices. Being a Christian to some people simply means adopting a lifestyle of abstaining from drinking, smoking, gambling, and not engaging in any devices that have sinful connotations. However, anyone who knows much about authentic Christianity, knows that although these are vices that one should not indulge himself in because they are unhealthy and unrighteous, yet the cessation of any or all of these vices cannot be used as a means of achieving one's salvation. If indeed one refrains from using these vices as a means of earning his salvation, his reform will most likely be short-lived because it would be energized by the flesh and not by the power of the Holy Spirit. Biblical conviction is formed by the Holy Spirit acting upon the Word of God in our lives. The Bible says in Psalm 119:9-11:

"Wherewithal shall a young man cleanse his way? by taking heed thereto according to thy word. With my

whole heart have I sought thee: O let me not wander from thy commandments. Thy word have I hid in mine heart, that I might not sin against thee."

The third reason why so many people are religious but not biblical in their position, is simply because *they do not have an intelligent faith about what Christianity is all about.*

Contrary to what many religious people believe, the Holy Spirit is not some mystical force that causes people to be out of control of themselves. But, rather, He is the Third Person of the Trinity that teaches the believer to exercise self-control as Galatians 5:22 & 23 tells us: ***"But the fruit of the Spirit is love, joy, peace, longsuffering, gentleness, goodness, faith, Meekness, temperance: against such there is no law."***

He, the Holy Spirit, also guides us into the truth. The Bible says in John 16:13:

"Howbeit when he, the Spirit of truth, is come, he will guide you into all truth: for he shall not speak of himself; but whatsoever he shall hear, that shall he speak: and he will shew you things to come."

Also, contrary to what many religious people believe, the purpose of the gospel preached from the pulpit is not designed to entertain them, but rather to rebuke God's people in their sins and to exhort the lost to salvation through Jesus Christ.

Finally, contrary to what so many religious people believe, the church does not exist as a mere social gathering or political forum, but is intended to be God's sanctuary for the saints to engage themselves in searching out the Scriptures to see whether the things they have learned are indeed true as the Bible has claimed. The Bible says in Acts 17:11:

"These were more noble than those in Thessalonica, in that they received the word with all readiness of mind, and searched the Scriptures daily, whether those things were so."

Yes, my beloved friend, one day there will be an accounting in judgement for the sole purpose of determining just how much of our earthly lives was wasted for being religious or just how much of it would be rewarded because we did it God's way. Notice these verses from God's Word:

"Every man's work shall be made manifest: for the day shall declare it, because it shall be revealed by fire; and the fire shall try every man's work of what sort it is. If any man's work abide which he hath built

thereupon, he shall receive a reward. If any man's work shall be burned, he shall suffer loss; but he himself shall be saved; yet so as by fire."

—I Corinthians 3:13-15

"For we must all appear before the judgement seat of Christ; that every one may receive the things done in his body, according to that he hath done, whether it be good or bad."

—II Corinthians 5:10

"I Did It My Way," by Frank Sinatra, may be a beloved song when sung before a throng of people here on earth, but the attitude that that song represents would indeed have dreadful consequences when we stand before the eternal Judge of the universe.

So, my fellow African-Americans, and Americans in general, let us humbly turn back to the God of Abraham, Isaac, and Jacob, and in the words of Tavis Smiley, "let's make Black America better."

"I think we
as a community
just need to be honest—
we are in trouble."

–Frank Melton
Mayor of Jackson, Mississippi

Chapter 3

The Crisis in Black America

* * * * * * *

When I read about the plight of God's covenant people in the Book of Hosea, I cannot but think about the crisis among black people today in their stride for freedom.

During the time of Hosea, the Israelites had not been for too long a people whom God had set free from the bondage of Egypt. They were God's chosen people who had been in captivity and had cried out to Jehovah God to set them free from the shackles of slavery. Their God heard their cry and delivered them from the tasks of their slave masters.

Having now been miraculously delivered out of Egypt, God then began to lead them through the wilderness to the promised land. However, He first had to teach them lessons in how to trust Him for their provisions. He wanted them to get a firsthand experience of how He could provide for them in their walk with Him if they obeyed His laws, and looked to Him in faith.

As an essential part of their training in the wilderness, God gave them His laws which they were to live by and to teach to their children (Deuteronomy 4:9). Concerning God's laws, they were explicitly told that obedience to the law of God would bring about blessings, but disobedience would bring down God's judgment upon them. ***"Behold, I set before you this day a blessing and a curse; a blessing, if ye obey the commandments of the LORD your God...and a curse, if ye will not obey the commandments of the LORD your God"*** (Deuteronomy 11:26-28). The evidence of this truth was repeatedly demonstrated to them, but they, being a stiffnecked people, continually disobeyed God's laws and oftentimes they suffered calamities and misfortunes at the hand of God.

Sometime later, Hosea, God's prophet, came upon the scene, and he too began to warn his people concerning God's judgment for rejecting the laws of God. We read in the book of Hosea these words: ***"My people are destroyed for lack of knowledge: because thou hast rejected knowledge, I will also reject thee, that thou shalt be no priest to me: seeing thou hast forgotten the law of thy God, I will also forget thy children. As they were increased, so they sinned against me: therefore will I change their glory into shame"*** (Hosea 4:6-7).

Notice here in this passage that Hosea warns the children of Israel of God's impending judgment that would come upon them for rejecting the laws of God. Because of Israel's pernicious ways, they would perish in the land.

Let me make an assertion here that is wise to take notice of, and that is, God is not a respecter of persons (Romans 2:11). Although the Israelites are God's covenant people, God did not spare them from His divine judgment that brought upon them grievous and painful suffering because they transgressed God's laws. The Holy Scripture tells us in Isaiah 55:11b that, ***"It*** [God's Word] ***shall not return unto me void, but it shall accomplish that which I please, and it shall prosper in the thing whereto I sent it."***

Let me hasten to say here, that if God allowed grievous suffering to come upon His own covenant people because they rebelled against the knowledge of God, that any people, be they black, white, or yellow, will perish in their ways and suffer much affliction if they choose to rebel against the laws of Almighty God.

As we look further at this passage, let us deal with Hosea's first admonition to the children of Israel. ***"...because thou hast rejected knowledge, I will also reject thee, that thou shalt be no priest to me..."*** (Hosea 4:6).

A Warning to Black America

As I read here about how God warned Israel, His covenant people, through the prophet Hosea, that He would reject them and they would no longer be His priest (people) because they rejected knowledge of His ways, I am reminded of the spiritual crisis in the African-American community. I believe that the words of Hosea spoken to His people in Biblical times are being echoed to Black America today — ***"My people are destroyed for lack of knowledge."***

Similarities Between African-Americans and the Israelites

I suppose that just as the Jews considered themselves to be "special" in the eyes of God, African-Americans also think of themselves as dear to the heart of God, as well, because they, too, have suffered as a people in this country. Had not Israel, God's covenant people, experienced a similar situation as slaves in the land of Egypt? And when the children of Israel cried out to their God concerning their affliction, did not God hear their cries and deliver them from bondage? What about African-Americans? Did not God hear the moanings and groanings of the African slaves and deliver them from bondage? Had not God demonstrated His bountiful love when He chose to intervene in this human tragedy and identify Himself with the poor, suffering African slaves as He had done for His covenant people, who had been in captivity in a strange land?

A Mutual Oversight

A salient fact that both the children of Israel and African-Americans seemed to have overlooked in their thinking was that, although God is a merciful and compassionate God Who identifies with the suffering of all people, He is also a righteous and just God Who does not wink at sin (Acts 17:30). God's holy laws are immutable, and whoever transgresses the laws of God must suffer divine judgment. ***"Be not deceived; God is not mocked: for whatsoever a man soweth, that shall he also reap"*** (Galatians 6:7).

As Hosea, God's prophet, warned the Israelites that calamity would come upon them and that they would perish in their ways because they transgressed God's laws and had rejected the laws of God, so shall it be for Black America as they, themselves, transgress God's holy and righteous laws, even though God has been very good to them.

Stride Toward Freedom

We, as blacks, in our "stride toward freedom" have committed the same atrocity as did God's covenant people. That is, we have turned our backs upon the very God who delivered us out of bondage. Throughout Biblical history, God constantly reminded Israel, in her journey to the "promised land," that He was the Lord God Who delivered them from out of the land of Egypt. This reminder was enunciated by God and the patriarchs of old. Why? Because Israel turned away from the law of God and went after idol gods. Israel, in her stride toward the "promised land," fell away into the sin of idolatry and turned away from God who had served as her Deliverer, Protector, and Provider in her pilgrimage to the land of "milk and honey."

The Crisis Among African-American People Today

As I ponder over Hosea's warning to the people of His day and learn how they forfeited the blessings of God because they rejected knowledge of God's laws, I cannot help but to think how we as blacks have transgressed God's holy laws and violated Scriptural principles in our stride toward the "promised land"—the place of freedom and blessing.

During the years following the Civil Rights Movement, it was apparent, even to the casual spectator, that blacks, in their struggle for justice and equality, were exceedingly blessed of God, in their struggle to be free and to gain their civil rights, which had been so long denied them. One may say that God had even opened up opportunities that we seemed hardly prepared for in those times. What had once seemed like it would take years to accomplish were quickly being achieved through Civil Rights legislation. Racial barriers that had stood for centuries were knocked down overnight. The only truthful explanation that anyone could offer for such mighty exploits was that God had gloriously intervened into this human drama and was manifesting His goodness upon the lives of a people who wholly feared and trusted in His sovereign grace for deliverance. God had heard our prayer, and had come to divinely rescue a people from their afflictions, as He had so done for the Jews, His chosen people.

An Unswerving Faith

We, as blacks, may not have had much of anything going on in our lives at that time worthy to embrace and cherish. However, no one could deny that we had an unswerving faith in the living God, and that He would vindicate a people who stood for a cause that was righteous and just. As a God of righteousness, God is pleased to vindicate a people who would trust in Him, and obey His holy laws. During those years, blacks revered and respected the laws of God. This is no longer the case.

A Forgotten Virtue

Today, it saddens my heart to have to say that this divine virtue has diminished in the lives of my people. Furthermore, I believe that the apathy that we as black people have, pertaining to God's holy and righteous laws, is an abomination in the eyes of God. Such apathy, I believe, has incurred God's judgment upon our people and has given rise to the many ills that plague African-Americans. God is never pleased with a people who have once been blessed and have tasted of His loving-kindness and then turn away from Him.

The words of Hosea are more evident in the lives of my people today than ever before: ***"My people are destroyed for lack of knowledge."*** But praise be unto God, there is still a way back if we would take heed to the writer of II Chronicles in chapter seven and verse fourteen: ***"If my people, which are called by my name, shall humble themselves, and pray, and seek my face, and turn from their wicked ways; then will I hear from heaven, and will forgive their sin, and heal their land."*** This powerful verse leads to my next chapter.

"If you are not as close to God as you used to be, who moved?"

–Author Unknown

Chapter 4
The Only Way Out

* * * * * * *

In the first three chapters of this book, I have outlined and delved into the problems and issues in the black community. But, my friend, we cannot continue to be a part of the problem, we must finally make a decision to be a part of the solution. In the words of Evangelist Daniel Whyte III, "the only somebody who can help us now is God." Here is the only way out for our people as it was for the children of Israel:

> ***"If my people, which are called by my name,***
> ***shall humble themselves, and pray,***
> ***and seek my face,***
> ***and turn from their wicked ways;***
> ***then will I hear from heaven,***
> ***and will forgive their sins,***
> ***and will heal their land."***
>
> —II Chronicles 7:14

Notice what this verse says and how it gives a solid solution to our problems as it did for the Israelites.

First of all, I want you to look at the fact that God is addressing **His people which are called by His Name.** This means that God expects **His people**, the people who claim to be God-followers in our communities, to take the first step and do what needs to be done:

1. **Humble Ourselves** — This means that we need to acknowledge the fact that we are "not all that," and that God is in charge. We need to follow Him, obey His Word, do His will and stop trying to make Him do our will.

2. **Pray!** — My friend, Daniel Whyte III, has a sermon that he preaches entitled, "A Praying Time." If there ever was a praying time, folks, that time is now! We need to commit ourselves to fasting and prayer for our community, and particularly for our young people. I appreciate what the great television host Tavis Smiley wrote in his book, ***The Covenant with Black America.*** But the truth of the matter is that after we do all that he and others have proposed, at the end of the day, **we must pray!**

   Much Prayer, Much Power!
   Little Prayer, Little Power!
   No Prayer, No Power!

   Not even "Black power" can save us now. There

are those in our community who think that we can turn things around without the help of God. But I am convinced that "only God can help us now." Therefore, we need to invite God into our dire situation through prayer.

3. **Seek My Face** — Not only do we, as a race of people, need to seek the face of God, but this entire nation, needs to seek the face of God lest we all be destroyed. We need to turn to God and repent of our sins and begin to show our love for Him by living for Him. Jesus said, ***"If you love me, keep my commandments"*** (John 14:15). He also said, ***"Why call ye me Lord, Lord; and do not the things which I say?"*** (Luke 6:46).

4. **And Turn From Our Wicked Ways** — God is calling upon us to turn from our crime, to turn from our robbery, to turn from our murder, to turn from our sin, and turn back to Him. May I lovingly encourage you, my fellow African-Americans, and, yea, America, to turn back to the God Who created us, Who loves us, and Who died for us, and then, ***He will hear from Heaven, forgive our sins, heal our land, and turn our shame back to glory!***

SEGUE

One of the main problems that I see in Black America is that we have what the Bible calls a *"form of Godliness"* but we *"deny the power thereof."* In other words, we have a lot of emotional religion, but little living out of that religion outside the church walls. Oftentimes, people go to church out of tradition, but they do not allow the church to change how they live on the outside. We are people who the Bible calls, *"Hearers of the word, but not doers of the word."* We have a religious faith, but not a biblical faith. This is the same problem that God had with the children of Israel—His chosen people. Many of the Israelites had fallen into a false religion as well as many of the priests of that day. And unfortunately, we have the same thing happening in the Black community today. Read On!

"Grace is free sovereign favor to the ill-deserving."

–Benjamin B. Warfield

Chapter 5
To Have an Intelligent Faith

* * * * * * *

Within minutes of talking to an individual about his or her salvation experience, I can usually tell whether such a person is biblically saved and trusting in the grace of God for salvation, or is still lost in his sins and trusting in good works to save him.

One may ask the question—How can anyone tell whether an individual is biblically saved or not, based upon such a brief encounter with that individual? My reply to you would be that it is not as difficult as it may seem to reach such a conclusion if one knows what the Bible has to say about biblical salvation.

What Biblical Salvation is Not

Before we take a look at what the Bible has to say about what biblical salvation is based upon, let us examine, first, what biblical salvation cannot be. Contrary to what many people believe, who in most cases do not possess an intelligent faith, biblical salvation is not based upon good works, nor good moral conduct, but rests entirely upon one's faith in the grace of God to save him. The thief, who died on the cross alongside Jesus Christ, is a good illustration of how the grace of God is bestowed upon a lost and dying sinner who was perishing in his sins. The thief, nailed helplessly to the cross, realized that within his own abilities, he could not save himself. Unlike Jesus, he was serving a just punishment for the crimes he had committed. Also, unlike Jesus, he did not have power at his disposal to come down from the cross if he so desired. No one took the life of Jesus. Jesus had power to lay down His life and to pick it up, but He chose to commit Himself to the cross for our sins. ***"Therefore doth my Father love me, because I lay down my life, that I might take it again. No man taketh it from me, but I lay it down of myself. I have power to lay it down, and I have power to take it again. This commandment have I received of my Father"*** (John 10:17-18).

The dying thief, realizing his inability to save himself from the horror and terror of his awful sins, knew he needed a Saviour—someone to save him from himself, someone to save him from the terrible consequence that awaited him after his death upon the cross. The thief knew within himself that he did not need the justice that was being served to him at that point, but what he needed in the eleventh hour of his life was someone who would show him mercy and grace at a time such as that.

The thief knew that the only hope of being saved throughout all eternity was for him to trust in the Lord Jesus Christ. This he did by casting himself at the mercy of Christ by asking Jesus to remember him when He entered into His kingdom. ***"And he said unto Jesus, Lord remember me when thou comest into thy kingdom*"** (Luke 23:42). Upon his request, the Lord Jesus immediately reached out to him and imputed to him the grace of God. What a marvelous demonstration of the grace of God Who looks beyond our faults and sees our need. Oh, the grace of God!

What is God's Grace?

The grace of God is His unmerited favor, which He freely bestows upon whosoever will. God's grace and His loving-kindness cannot be earned; neither is it merited by anyone's righteous acts, but it is freely given to all who believe in the Lord Jesus Christ. Therefore, any work or effort rendered to obtain salvation is futile in the eyes of God. Thus, any attempt on the part of unregenerate man to perform good works or deeds to merit his salvation is a total disgust and an abomination to the Lord.

The prophet Isaiah, in Isaiah 64:6 had this to say about depraved mankind who would offer good works to a holy and righteous God as a means of deserving salvation: ***"But we are all as an unclean thing, and all our righteousnesses are as filthy rags; and we all do fade as a leaf; and our iniquities, like the wind, have taken us away."***

The New Testament saint, the Apostle Paul, preached to the Galatian church that any attempt to present good works as a means to achieve salvation is merely to "frustrate" the grace of God. ***"I do not frustrate the grace of God: for if righteousness come by the law, then Christ is dead in vain"*** (Galatians 2:21). According to the Apostle Paul, our salvation rests entirely upon the mercy and grace of God to save us, and is not based upon any works of our own be they good works or bad works. Salvation is a gift of God. No one could attest to this truth any more than the Apostle Paul who declared himself on one hand to have been a Pharisee who adhered to the keeping of the Jewish laws in the stricter sense. ***"Though I might also have confidence in the flesh. If any other man thinketh that he hath whereof he might trust in the flesh, I more: Circumcised the eighth day, of the stock of Israel, of the tribe of Benjamin, an Hebrew of the Hebrews; as touching the law, a Pharisee; Concerning zeal, persecuting the***

church; touching the righteousness which is in the law, blameless" (Philippians 3:4-6).

However, on the other hand, Apostle Paul had declared himself to be chief among sinners who once had a mission to persecute Christians. He was on a mission then on the Damascus Road when the sovereign grace of God struck him off his horse, not to kill him, but to gloriously save him. Oh, the grace of God that still saves wretched sinners even today while we are running contrary to the will of God.

The Lord Jesus, during His earthly ministry, served this notice upon all those who had in mind using good works and some other means of entering the kingdom of Heaven other than by the grace of God: ***"Verily, verily, I say unto you, he that entereth not by the door*** [Christ] ***into the sheepfold, but climbeth up some other way, the same is a thief and a robber"*** (John 10:1).

My friend, only the grace of God—God's loving-kindness—God's free gift, can truly equip one for entering into the kingdom of Heaven. Are you today relishing in God's grace or perishing in your good works?

Good Works Cannot Merit Salvation

If you talk to the average church member about how he became a Christian, more than likely he will give you a resume of all his outstanding works. Chances are, you will hear him say something that is mentioned here in this context: I am a good husband or wife (whatever the case); I do not run around on my mate; I try to bring up my children the right way; I am a good neighbour; I do not bother anyone, and I attend to my own business.

However, if it still appears that you are still not convinced his salvation experience is a valid one, then, he would begin to inundate you with religious services he has performed in his church such as: I was brought up in the church; I sing in the choir; I am a Sunday school teacher; I am a member of the Usher Board; I am on the Missionary Board; I was baptized at an early age; I go to church practically every Sunday.

Ignorance of what Biblical Salvation is all About

The person who is ignorant of what biblical salvation is all about does not know that the very argument he uses to support his Christian experience is the very reason the Bible gives for a person who is not biblically saved. I suppose that one of the most frequently used passages of the Bible that soul-winners and Christian workers alike use in witnessing to individuals and winning the lost to Jesus is found in Ephesians 2:8-9: ***"For by grace are ye saved through faith and that not of yourselves; it is a gift of God: Not of works, lest any man should boast."***

Notice that in these verses, we are told that we are saved through God's grace (loving-kindness) imputed to us by exercising our faith in God. Let us examine these scriptures for further enlightenment:

1. First, notice that in these two verses, the issue of salvation is being discussed here in the term: ***"For by grace are ye saved."***

2. Second, we are told that the way we are saved is by no means of our own efforts or our own doings. This is stated in the clause: ***"...that (salvation) not of yourselves."***

3. Third, we are reminded again that salvation is not achieved by our own efforts. It is a gift bestowed upon us by God. This is made clear in the statement: ***"it is a gift of God."***

4. Fourth, in verse nine of this chapter, we are told explicitly and succinctly that salvation takes place without any works of our own. This is necessary for the express purpose of denying

> anyone any pleasure of boasting about having any part in the salvation experience. This truth is stated in the expression: *"Not of works lest any man should boast."*

Now, when I am inquiring of someone concerning his salvation experience and that person begins to relate to me all about how he was saved through his noble works and his lofty deeds, I know that such a person is not only biblically ignorant, but he is also biblically unsaved. Anyone who is an heir of the grace of God certainly would not be declaring his position on how he has earned his salvation when the Bible teaches that salvation is a gift.

Ironically, the person who claims good works as a means of deserving his salvation does not know that he is serving an indictment upon himself as not being truly saved and one who has not been born into the family of God. Thus, this person is still lost in his sins, and furthermore, has been deceived in his thinking to embrace a false salvation.

Biblical Salvation is a Gift

Biblical salvation, as it is presented in the Bible, is a gift bestowed upon us by God when we put our faith in Jesus Christ, God's Son. It is not a transformation that takes place by working for it nor by trying to earn it by our own merits, but simply by putting our faith in the finished work of Jesus Christ who proclaimed from the cross some 2,000 years ago, ***"It is finished"*** (John 19:30). My friend, you don't have to work for it; you just have to accept what Christ has already done.

Salvation as a gift has already been purchased and paid for through the shed blood of our Saviour. Although it is a free gift to all who would dare to receive it, it cost God His only Son as payment for our sins. "***For God so loved the world, that He gave his only begotten Son, that whosoever believeth in him should not perish, but have everlasting life"*** (John 3:16).

Won't you trust Him today as Saviour and Lord by standing on the phrase: *"Nothing to the cross I bring,/ Simply to the cross I cling,/ Grace, grace, God's marvelous grace!"*

"If the society today allows wrongs to go unchallenged, the impression is created that those wrongs have the approval of the majority."

–Barbara Jordan

Chapter 6
An Intelligent Faith is a Practical Faith

* * * * * * *

Having now been a Christian for nearly thirty years, it is still disturbing to me to realize that I lingered for quite a while before making a conscious decision about becoming a Christian because I had perceived Christianity as a religion which was not based upon practicality. I wish that I could say that such a negative perception was based upon some illusion of my own personal experience, which I had conjured up in my own imagination, but that was certainly not the case. The case was, however, that I had allowed the experiences of some other so-called Christians to distort my view of the God of the Bible.

An Erroneous View of the God of the Bible

As I think back upon those years, I know now that my perception of the God of the Bible was not based upon any research or my own investigation of the Holy Scripture. It saddens me to say that during this time, I had not even so much as attempted to read the Bible for myself, and yet I allowed the experiences and the opinions of others to form my views concerning the God of the Bible.

A Tragic Mistake by Many

Today, as I encounter many people in my walk through life, I often come across those persons who are misguided in their thinking and thus, have formed a negative view of the God of the Bible. Their view of God is wholly based upon the opinions of other people. These inferences are always faulty, and to say the least, most ridiculous. Yet, many of these dear people would rather hold to their false beliefs than read the Bible and search out these things to see if they are true.

Let us serve notice here, that whenever Jesus Christ came upon such persons with false doctrines and those who embraced a faith that was unintelligent and impractical, He challenged them to search the Scriptures, to see for themselves, if those things were true in which they were believing. He said: ***"Search the scriptures; for in them ye think ye have eternal life: and they are they which testify of me"*** (John 5:39). Furthermore, Acts 17:11 states: ***"These were more noble than those in Thessalonica, in that they received the word with all readiness of mind, and searched the scriptures daily,***

whether those things were so." It is a tragedy that over the years, many dear souls have ended up in hell because they refused to search the Scriptures for themselves and change their views of the true and living God.

How then is a Christian's Faith Practical

We started out by saying that the reason I lingered in becoming a Christian was because I did not relate to Christians as being practical. That is to say, from what I had observed, from the experiences of other so-called Christians, I did not see any practical value of being a Christian in this life. Although as an unsaved person, I had no problem with accepting the fact that there would be a better life for the Christian when he passed into eternity, yet, it was disturbing to me to believe that being a Christian in this life was not something that I could look forward to becoming because it seemed not to offer any hope, any help, any relief, any protection, nor any joy.

Let me hasten to say here, oh, how wrong I was. Since I have become a Christian, I know now that the Christian faith is alive and well, and yes, very practical. How wonderful it is to be set free from the ignorant devices of Satan's lies. Please allow me in the remainder of this writing to share with you just a few ways in which being a Christian is practical:

1. **As a Christian, I can relate to God as my Heavenly Father**. In today's society, not many of us can boast of having an earthly father whom we think well of, and know that he is always with us and will never leave us in times of distress, or in times of grief. You name it, and our Heavenly Father is right there for us. In His own words, He says, ***"I will never leave thee, nor forsake thee"*** (Hebrews 13:5b). Just how many Christians do you know today who can testify concerning these truths in regard to their Heavenly Father?

2. **As a Christian, I can relate to God as my Provider**. As we come to know the God of the Bible, we cannot but get to know Him as our Jehovah-Jireh—the God Who provides. It is God's nature, it is God's essence, it is God's name and reputation to provide for His people. I cannot begin to tell you just how many times I have had to look to God to provide the essential things in this life. I relish in the promise: ***"But my God shall supply all your need according to his riches in glory by Christ Jesus"*** (Philippians 4:19).

3. **As a Christian, I can relate to God as my Friend**. In the kind of self-serving society we live in today, you

and I must be careful in choosing a friend. If our TV talk shows are any kind of representation of what goes on in real life, then we are all doomed when it comes to having a true friend. What we see on many of the popular TV shows are friends betraying each other, friends taking the mates of their best friends, and friends, whose ulterior motive is just to exploit their own personal gains. It behooves one to take notice of the lyrics of the hymn sung in many of our churches today: "*There's not a friend like the lowly Jesus/No not one, No not one.*"

Yes, beloved, my favorite hymn which I often sing when I feel the need of a close friend to share my inner most thoughts and feelings is the song, "*What a Friend We Have in Jesus.*" I know that in Jesus there is someone that sticketh closer than a brother (Proverbs 18:24). Oh, yes! being a Christian is not just a hope for the future, but it is a living faith that has much practical value for this life as well.

"Salvation causes us to step out of sin's slavery into security with Christ."

–Selected

Chapter 7
Not Brainwashed, but Bloodwashed

* * * * * * *

Within the black community, we have come to believe that the reason why there are some blacks who tend to adopt a certain viewpoint about sensitive moral or social issues is because they have been brainwashed with a "white mentality." This, of course, is intended to stigmatize those blacks with a kind of negative profile as the ones who cannot be trusted when it comes to having the right perspective regarding sensitive social or moral issues.

The stigma of having a "white mentality" implies that this is someone who has developed a negative self–image of being black, due to years of being oppressed by a white racist system that indoctrinated him to believe that everything about being black is inferior, and everything about being white is superior. Thusly, such a person comes to believe this damnable lie and subsequently, acquires the same kind of mentality that whites also adopt when it comes to anything pertaining to blacks. It is therefore believed that such blacks can no longer be expected to relate to issues as other blacks perceive them, but tend to view them in the same respect that whites regard them.

A Sad Commentary

It is a sad commentary, but nonetheless, the truth, that there are a number of blacks who we can say may have been brainwashed by an oppressive white system that has caused them to view issues differently than the average black within the black culture. However, this is not the case with all blacks, neither with most blacks, especially if these blacks are Christians and hold true to their faith.

Blacks Devoted to Racial Heritage

There is a widening schism between those blacks who are devoted to their racial heritage and those who are devoted to their Christian heritage.

Those blacks who are devoted to their racial heritage are not willing to compromise, nor change their stand on moral or social issues, if, for some reason, the issue has some racial implications. The validity of an issue is rarely seen from a right or wrong perspective, but it is decided upon how it would affect the overall welfare of the black community. If for some reason, the issue is perceived as portraying blacks in a negative light which could further cause whites to malign the image of blacks, racial motives will then become the most compelling reason why these blacks would have chosen this course of action; thus, what is true, what is right, and what is moral will be sacrificed upon the altar of race and black pride.

Blacks Devoted to Christian Heritage

Unlike those blacks who would sacrifice truth and morality at the altar of racial heritage, there are also within the black community those blacks who are born–again believers who are devoted to the Christian faith. Because these blacks are guided by their biblical convictions more so than by their allegiance to race pride, often times, these black Christians are the ones who other blacks refer to as being "brainwashed" or having a "white mentality". They are thought to be "brainwashed" by the white system because they tend to view an issue differently than their black counterparts.

For instance, the issue of crime and drugs within the black community would probably be seen by those blacks who are devoted to racial heritage as a conspiracy by the U.S. Government to exterminate black people. Racial profiling, police brutality and other destructive measures are all conditions, they say, calculated to bring about the destruction of innocent black people.

Those blacks who are devoted to the Christian faith would tend to see the crime and drug problems within the black community from a different perspective. They would recognize crime and drugs as a manifestation of sin and wickedness that befall a people who have turned their feet from the way of righteousness. They believe the only way back to a life of prosperity, peace, and God's blessings is through II Chronicles 7:14: ***"If my people which are called by my name, shall humble themselves, and pray, and seek my face, and turn from their wicked ways; then will I hear from heaven and will forgive their sin and will heal their land."***

These are those blacks who believe that ***"righteousness exalteth a nation, but sin is a reproach to any people."*** (Proverbs 14:31).

Not Brainwashed, but Bloodwashed

It is true that blacks who practice genuine Christianity do indeed perceive things differently because they tend to see things from a divine perspective rather than from a secular perspective. They cannot be considered brainwashed by a white racist system or by a black militant system. But rather, they have been "bloodwashed" through the life transforming power of the death and resurrection of Jesus Christ and thus, they are renewed in their spirits and in their minds (Ephesians 4: 22–25).

These are the kind of Christians whose faith reflects genuine Christianity because they embrace a faith based on true love. Scripture tells us that true followers of Christ are to embrace a love that does not harm one's neighbour (Romans 13:10). That neighbour, my friend, could very well be someone who hates me, despitefully uses me, discriminates against me, disrespects me, and may have in the past, tried to rob me of my human dignity. But if I am going to be genuine in my Christianity, I must forgive him as Christ Jesus has also forgiven me of my trespasses.

> ***"And forgive us our debts, as we forgive our debtors...For if ye forgive men their trespasses, your heavenly Father will also forgive you: But if ye forgive not men their trespasses, neither will your heavenly Father forgive your trespasses."***
>
> –Matthew 6:12, 14-15

No, my friend, we are not "brainwashed," but "***bloodwashed***," and we praise God for it — Hallelujah!

"As long as you are tangled in wrong and revenge, blow and counterblow, aggression and defense, you will be constantly drawn into fresh wrong...Only forgiveness frees us from the injustice of others."

–Romano Guardini

Chapter 8

The Need for Blacks to Forgive those Guilty of the Sin of Prejudice and Racism

Chapter 8
The Need for Blacks to Forgive those Guilty of the Sin of Prejudice and Racism

* * * * * * *

Permit me to begin this discussion by addressing the concerns of those who feel that blacks have every right to have hatred and bitterness in their hearts toward the white community for having afflicted them with the pains of prejudice and racism in the past.

A Legitimate Cause for Hate and Bitterness?

There are some blacks who strongly feel that they have a legitimate cause for hate and bitterness toward those whites who have afflicted upon them the pains of racism in the past. It is said that some blacks have even practiced reverse discrimination. But the question I want to ask is: *Just because they think they have a cause to hate, does that make it ethical for them to do so?*

You see, just because one has a legal right to commit an act does not necessarily mean that it is the ethical thing to do. Let me further illustrate this point in the same context which black people themselves have been victimized by just that kind of ploy. At one time slavery was legal in this country, particularly in the South where African blacks were sold as slaves at the slave market. But we know, today, that it was unethical and de-humanizing. However, none of this made it illegal. Whites still had the legal rights to purchase slaves who were being auctioned at the slave markets.

Now, I know that there are some blacks who would want to reverse the time, and see whites placed in the same kind of humiliating predicament; to see them suffer as blacks suffered. Maybe to some blacks this would be just what they deserved. But I, myself, would not want to see such a fate befall any people. Slavery, in any setting, where one man becomes another man's property, is immoral and de-humanizing. It is the worst kind of human suffering.

Slavery, Prejudice and Racism are Ungodly

Throughout the ages, slavery, prejudice and racism have been used as the most effective instrument in the hands of mortal man to crush the spirit of his fellow man and to rob him of his human dignity. No people, neither has any individual, gone unscathed from the tentacles of its devastating grips. Once in the jaws of prejudice and racism, one's emotion and self-esteem are crushed and indelibly stained with the seeds of bitterness and resentment that root itself within the soul of man. And the only deliverance from such a traumatic experience as prejudice and racism can only be exercised through a divine spiritual experience.

True Christian Salvation is the Best Remedy for Racial Prejudice

Oftentimes, we hear of different workshops and seminars being offered to those who want to deal with their racism and those who have been victimized by racial prejudice. The technique often used in these therapeutic sessions is for the individual to engage in role-play and act out his fears and hostility. The only things I have ever seen come out of these workshops were more frustrations and more vexing of the spirit because the problems of racism were so deep-seated until it had scarred the psyche and the soul of man. Therefore, a conversion experience seems to be the only plausible solution for the remedy of prejudice and racism.

Why is it then that a divine conversion experience would seem to be the only remedy for deliverance from racism and prejudice? I will tell you why. Because prejudice and racism are deeply rooted in sin, it would require a divine spiritual experience to eradicate the sin of prejudice.

The Twin Sins of Prejudice and Racism

Notice that I said the "sins of prejudice and racism" because prejudice is a sin, and sin is any act that transgresses the law of God. And prejudice clearly transgresses the law of God. The law of God teaches that we should not hold respect of one person over another.

The writer, James, puts it this way: ***"My brethren, have not the faith of our Lord Jesus Christ, the Lord of glory, with respect of persons. For if there come unto your assembly a man with a gold ring, in goodly apparel, and there come in also a poor man in vile raiment; And ye have respect to him that weareth the gay clothing, and say unto him, Sit thou here in a good place; and say to the poor, Stand thou there, or sit here under my footstool: Are ye not then partial in yourselves, and are become judges of evil thoughts?"***

—James 2:1-4

Notice here that in this scenario, the act that evoked the sin of prejudice was determined on the basis of how the individual was dressed. And because one individual was considered to be dressed in better clothing than the other, he was shown preferential treatment. He was judged to be rich and consequently was treated differently than his fellow man who was considered poor.

In the minds of some people, I suppose they would find the act of discrimination here to be somewhat ludicrous since it was based upon how the individual was dressed. Well, let me hasten to say here, not only is this ludicrous, but in the eyes of God, any act of discrimination, racism and prejudice is an abomination. It is also blatant sin.

In the eyes of God, it does not matter whether one is discriminated against because of the kind of clothing he wears or the culture he happens to belong to. God holds no respect of persons and He expects the same from us because we are all made in the image of God, and any ungodly and prejudicial reason which would cause us to discriminate against our neighbour, violates the royal law of God. We are to love our neighbour as we do ourselves. ***"If ye fulfill the royal law according to the scripture, Thou shalt love thy neighbour as thyself, ye do well"*** (James 2:8). And not to do so, is to clearly transgress the holy law of God.

Why Blacks Must Forgive Those Guilty of Racism

One might wonder, why should blacks as a people learn

to forgive those guilty of the sin of racism when we are not the ones who have practiced racism against the white race? I will tell you why. Although we ourselves have been the victims of racial prejudice, still we transgress God's law if we do not forgive people when they have transgressed against us.

As Christians, the Holy Scripture reminds us throughout the Bible to forgive those who have sinned against us. And we have already established that prejudice and racism are sins in the sight of God. I suppose the teaching of the Scripture where most Christians are familiar with in reference to forgiving those who have transgressed against us is in the passage we often refer to as *The Lord's Prayer:* ***"And forgive us our debt as we forgive our debtors"*** (Matthew 6:12). Also in verse fourteen of this same chapter, we are again reminded of how we should deal with this particular offense in relation to our Christian conduct and responsibility. In this passage, the writer clearly and precisely states it in this manner: ***"For if ye forgive men their trespasses, your heavenly Father will also forgive your trespasses."***

These passages explicitly command Christians to forgive, if God, Himself, is going to forgive us our sins. So, it is of utmost importance that we, as a people, learn to forgive those whites and the racist system that have blatantly discriminated against us if we expect and desire

God's blessings upon our lives as individuals and as a race of people.

So, despite all of the untold sufferings we have been afflicted with because of racism, still God in all His righteousness and holy ways, just cannot sanctify and bestow His blessings upon a people who cannot find it within their hearts to forgive their fellowman who has unjustly persecuted them.

Dear Christian friend, let us not let the unsaved world mold us into their ungodly ways, but rather, let us be the light of the world to expose their darkness, and the salt of the earth to retard corruption, so on that day, when we stand before our Lord to give an account, we shall be glad that our living was not in vain. Amen!

"In every conceivable manner, the family is a link to our past, and a bridge to our future."

–Alex Haley

Chapter 9
The Need for a Strong Black Family

****

A while back, I received a study guide booklet entitled *The Strong Family*. According to the views of the author, Chuck Swindoll, the strong family is quickly, today, becoming an endangered species. He writes, "The world is different today, and the challenge of keeping the genuine Christian family from becoming an 'endangered species' is perhaps more difficult now than it has ever been. That's the bad news."

The good news, Mr. Swindoll goes on to say, is that the biblical principles for raising a family have not changed. But there is one requirement on our part—**authenticity**. Only those families whose faith is genuine will survive. So, if we are going to meet the challenge before us—that of building genuine Christian families—we must keep it real– authenticity.

The Essentials of Authenticity

Mr. Swindoll contends in his article that as the Israelites prepared to enter the Promised Land, they too faced an intimidating challenge—to penetrate the pagan culture. Israel was moving into a new stage of their existence as a nation. The first had been slavery in Egypt. The second was the stage of wilderness wanderings. Now they were about to move into a period unlike anything they had known before. To prepare them for this challenge, Moses gathered the Israelites, and gave them the essentials of an authentic faith, that would not only help their families to survive, but their nation to survive as well.

Four Essentials of Authentic Faith

1. The first essential of an authentic faith for the Israelites and for black America as well, is for us to love God with all of our heart, mind, and soul. For Israel to survive successfully in the land, parents had to be permeated by a love for God. Notice with me the Word of God on this matter:

"***Now these are the commandments, the statutes, and the judgements which the Lord your God commanded to teach you, that you might do them in the land wither ye go to possess it: That thou mighest fear the Lord thy God, to keep all his statutes and his commandments, which I command thee, thou, and thy son, and thy son's son, all the days of thy life; and that*** *thy days may be prolonged. Hear therefore, O Israel, and observe to do it; that it may be well with thee...Hear, O Israel: The Lord our God is one Lord: and thou shalt love the Lord thy God with all thine heart, and with all thy soul, and with all thy might"* (Deuteronomy 6:1–5).

Notice in this passage it was essential for parents to pass down to their posterity a reverential fear and a deep and abiding love for their wonderful God. It was of the utmost importance for the generation of their posterity to possess knowledge of loving, serving, and worshipping God and God alone. This kind of all-encompassing love for God is an authentic and genuine faith, to be passed down to their children and grandchildren.

2. The second essential of an authentic faith is regarding the truth of God's Word. For there to be an authentic faith in the Christian home, the parents must consistently pass down God's truth to their children. But first, the parents must have that truth in their own hearts.

"And these words, which I command thee this day, shall be in thine heart: And thou shalt teach them diligently unto thy children, And shalt talk of them when thou sittest in thine house, and when thou

walkest by the way, and when thou liest down, and when thou risest up" (Deuteronomy 6:6–7).

Let us notice here something that is of utmost significance. When we are transferring our faith to our children; it must be seen as true and authentic in accordance with the Word of God, otherwise, we will be seen as imposters having betrayed our faith in Christ, who is the embodiment of true Christianity.

Much of society today reflects a superficial faith in Christianity. Much of the reason we are witnessing such turmoil in society today, results from having a superficial faith in regard to Christianity.

Today's generation of youth have witnessed too much of a disparity between that which they have observed in the lives of professing Christians in their homes, and the lessons taught to them in their Sunday School classes, and the message preached to them from the pulpit in Sunday morning services. Thus, many of them have come to see the entire Christian faith as being nothing but a farce.

Above all else, the home should be a place where an authentic faith is both nurtured and practiced in accordance with the Word of God.

3. The third essential of an authentic faith is regarding our response toward affluence. The Israelites experienced much temptation when they entered Canaan, the land of milk and honey. Notice with me in the Word of God:

"And it shall be, when the Lord thy God shall have brought thee into the land which he sware unto thy fathers...to give thee great and goodly cities, which thou buildest not, And houses full of all good things, which thou filledst not,...when thou shalt have eaten and be full; Then beware lest thou forget the Lord, which brought thee forth out of the land of Egypt, from the house of bondage. Thou shalt fear the Lord thy God, and serve him...Ye shall not go after other gods of the gods of the people which are round about you" (Deuteronomy 6: 10–14).

The Israelites would go from an impoverished life in the wilderness to a wealthy life in Canaan—from a life of manna to a land flowing with milk and honey. But notice that the Lord's advice to them in the midst of such affluence is to remind them not to forget to honor the Lord as the true source of their blessings.

4. The fourth essential ingredient for families to be strong and to possess an authentic faith is to acquire "a tender, humble heart of gratitude for God's

blessings."

Oh, how often do we see this kind of attitude prevailing in the lives of God's people today. We are too quick to forget the lesson the Psalmist proclaims in Psalm 103:2: ***"Bless the Lord, O my soul, and forget not his benefits."***

If African-American families are going to survive as strong families in today's society, we must have an authentic faith.

"It is in the process of being worshipped that God communicates His presence to men."

–C. S. Lewis

Chapter 10
Worshipping God with an Intelligent Faith

* * * * * * *

"O come, let us sing unto the Lord: let us make a joyful noise to the rock of our salvation. Let us come before his presence with thanksgiving, and make a joyful noise unto him with psalms. For the Lord is a great God, and a great King above all gods. In his hands are the deep places of the earth: the strength of the hills is his also. The sea is his, and he made it: and his hands formed the dry land. O come, let us worship and bow down: let us kneel before the Lord our maker. For he is our God; and we are the people of his pasture, and the sheep of his hand. To day, if ye will hear his voice, Harden not your heart, as in the provocation, and as in the day of temptation in the wilderness."

—Psalm 95:1-8

I would like to say at the beginning of this final essay, that perhaps you have wondered time and time again as you have hurriedly gotten dressed on a Sunday morning to come to worship, just why it is that we sense the urgency to do so. And yet, Sunday after Sunday, we faithfully attend worship service because somehow, we believe deeply within our inner man, that God is pleased when we come into the House of the Lord to worship Him. The psalmist David said: ***"I was glad when they said unto me, Let us go into the house of the Lord"*** (Psalm 122:1).

God Has Ordained Worship

So now we know that God would have us to set aside a time in our lives just for us to worship Him. We are reminded throughout the Bible to give occasion to this event because it plays such a vital part in our communion with God and also serves as a time of fellowship with those of the household of faith.

The Bible Exhorts Us to Worship

The Bible not only exhorts us to worship, but God also gives us precise instructions as to how we are to worship Him. Believers are taught in the Scriptures to worship God "in spirit and in truth." ***"God is a Spirit: and they that worship him must worship him in spirit and in truth"*** (John 4:24). He also exhorts us not to miss meeting together for worship by stating: "***Not forsaking the assembling of ourselves together, as the manner of some is; but exhorting one another: and so much the more, as ye see the day approaching"*** (Hebrews

10:25). The expressed purpose behind this command is to provide an occasion for believers to worship collectively.

God is Concerned About How we Worship

I want to say to you, God has some thoughts concerning how we should worship and He wants you to hear them. So, today, if you will hear His voice in this writing, harden not your heart.

Historical Background to Psalm 95

Psalm ninety-five is a coronation psalm written by David and adapted for the dedication of the second temple during the time when Israel was being re-gathered and was coming out of Babylon's captivity. The movement culminated in the rebuilding of the temple in Jerusalem. During this time in Israel's history, it was an occasion of celebration because Israel had been in captivity for seventy years. And once again, God had proven Himself faithful in delivering her out of bondage. Another reason for this being a time of celebration for Israel was because God had pardoned them for their sin of idolatry and had restored them back into His good graces. And if we as black Americans will turn back to God, even in these dark days, He will pardon our sins, bring us back into

His good graces, and turn our **shame to glory**.

Relating to Israel's Celebration

Permit me to say, if you would, that I can truly relate to the rejoicing spirit of the children of Israel, because I, too, know what it is like to be set free from the captivity of bondage. Although my bondage cannot be thought of as being in physical captivity, but I tell you, as a depraved sinner, Satan had my mind, my spirit and my soul in captivity. I thank God for having saved me and set me free from the burden of my sins. Today, I am still rejoicing in the liberties of Christ, for, ***"If the Son therefore shall make you free, ye shall be free indeed"*** (John 8:36).

A Psalm of Praise and Adoration

Psalm ninety-five is a psalm of praise and adoration written to instruct and exhort Israel to worship God in a manner and fashion pleasing to Jehovah God. The children of Israel needed instruction in how to worship and serve the Lord in the holy temple. The children of Israel needed to learn in their worship experience that God, in His holiness, will not accept anything less than true worship.

Many Christians Today are Ignorant Concerning True Worship

In many of our churches today, Christians are ignorant concerning biblical worship. They are worshipping God in their own self-styled manner. To some Christians, their attitude concerning worship is no more than to routinely show up for Sunday morning service without any regard as to what goes on in the worship service.

To others, worship service is centered around praising and extolling some preacher who entertains his congregation by whooping and hollering and running around in the pulpit. And then there are those churches which are becoming more popular among Christians today whose worship services consist of gospel choirs reeling and rocking all down the aisles, healing and deliverance services lasting for hours and culminating with "slaying worshippers in the spirit."

Sad to say, although these Christians may be sincere in their worship devotion, yet none of these experiences are what the Bible teaches concerning biblical worship. True biblical worship is not centered around exalting man, but extolling and experiencing God. God alone is only to be worshipped and praised.

How Then Shall We Worship?

Let us look at Psalm ninety-five for what biblical or true worship is all about:

1. *True worship is when we come into the sanctuary and acclaim and celebrate God as Lord.* ***"O come, let us sing unto the Lord: let us make a joyful noise to the rock of our salvation"*** (Psalm 95:1). The children of Israel had to be taught a profound truth that when they went into the temple to worship God, they needed to be reminded that they were in the presence of the Lord their God who had delivered them out of captivity. He was their rock of salvation and their rock of safety.

   When we, today, as God's people, come into the sanctuary to worship God, we need to be also in a celebrating mood as Israel, rejoicing in our spirit that Christ is not only our Rock of salvation, but He is a very present help in the time of trouble. ***"God is our refuge and strength, a very present help in trouble"*** (Psalm 46:1).

2. *True worship is the offering of a sacrifice of praise and thanksgiving unto the Lord.* ***"Let us come before his presence with thanksgiving and***

make a joyful noise unto him with psalms" (Psalm 95:2). The children of Israel needed to know that when they went into the temple to worship God, their hearts should be filled with gratitude and thanksgiving remembering where the Lord had brought them from. When we as Christians today, come into the house of the Lord, we too, need to be singing praises to Him because we are remembering the good hand of the Lord. ***"O taste and see that the Lord is good, blessed is the man that trusteth in him"*** (Psalm 34:8).

3. *True worship exhorts us to be mindful of God's majesty.* ***"For the Lord is a great God, and a great King above all gods"*** (Psalm 95:3). The children of Israel needed to understand and to rejoice in the truth that when they come into the temple to worship God that He is King of kings and Lord of lords.

   We, too, as Christians, need to acclaim Christ as King of kings and Lord of lords. We need to see Him in all His majesty as Isaiah saw Him in the temple "high and lifted up," and understanding that we do not deserve to be in the glory of His presence.

4. *True worship is when we learn to rejoice in the knowledge that Jehovah God is the Creator of all things.* ***"In his hand are the deep places of the earth: the strength of the hill is his also. The sea is his, and he made it: And his hands formed the dry land"*** (Psalm 95:4-5). Israel needed to know in their attitude of worship that Elohim, the Creator of the universe, was more than their covenant God who delivered them out of captivity, but He was also the God of all flesh and the God of all creation.

   We as Christians, today, also need to celebrate God as Creator of all things, the Giver of Life, and the Sustainer of the Universe when we come into the sanctuary to worship Him.

5. Finally, *true and biblical worship culminates in hearing the voice of God and taking heed to how He wants us to worship Him.* Israel needed to understand how they worshipped God, had a direct correlation to how they would serve Him. The children of Israel, in their past history, had provoked God in the wilderness because they made themselves idols and served not the true, living God. God's guideline for worshipping Him is the same today as always. ***"They that worship***

Him must worship Him in spirit and in truth." (John 4:24).

If we as African-Americans are going to get back on track, not only should our families have an authentic faith, but our worship should be authentic as well. God is still speaking to His people today concerning worshipping Him with an intelligent faith. Today, "if you will hear His voice, harden not your heart."

STOP THE VIOLENCE!

A RESOLUTION TO GET INVOLVED

WHEN SOME FEW OF US
CONTROL THE MOST OF US
THEN IT IS TIME
FOR THE REST OF US
TO GET INVOLVED
BEFORE THE FEW
MAKE IT BAD
FOR ALL OF US

-SAMUEL L. MADISON

From Shame to Glory

The first step in turning our "shame back to glory" is accepting Christ as our Saviour. If you have not done so already, please hear what my friend, Daniel Whyte III, has to say about this important subject. God has used him to see thousands come to know Christ as Saviour, and he can help you find Christ as well:

1. **Accept the fact that you are a sinner, and that you have broken God's law**.

   The Bible says in Ecclesiastes 7: 20: "***For there is not a just man upon earth that doeth good, and sinneth not***."

   Romans 3:23: "***For all have sinned and come short of the glory of God.***"

2. **Accept the fact that there is a penalty for sin**. The Bible states in Romans 6:23: "***For the wages of sin is death...***"

3. **Accept the fact that you are on the road to hell**. Jesus Christ said in Matthew 10:28: "***And fear not them which kill the body, but are not able to kill***

the soul: but rather fear him which is able to destroy both soul and body in hell."

The Bible says in Revelation 21:8: "***But the fearful, and unbelieving, and the abominable, and murderers, and whoremongers and sorcerers, and idolaters, and all liars, shall have their part in the lake which burneth with fire and brimstone: which is the second death***."

4. **Accept the fact that you cannot do anything to save yourself!**

   The Bible states in Ephesians 2: 8, 9: ***"For by grace are ye saved through faith: and that not of yourselves: it is a gift of God. Not of works, lest any man should boast."***

5. **Accept the fact that God loves you more than you love yourself, and that He wants to save you from hell.**

   "***For God so loved the world, that He gave his only begotten Son, that whosoever believeth in Him should not perish, but have everlasting life."*** (Jesus Christ, John 3:16).

6. **With these facts in mind, please repent of your sins,**

believe on the Lord Jesus Christ and pray and ask Him to come into your heart and save you this very moment.

The Bible states in the book of Romans 10:9, 13: "***That if thou shalt confess with thy mouth the Lord Jesus, and shalt believe in thine heart that God hath raised him from the dead, thou shalt be saved." "For whosoever shall call upon the name of the Lord shall be saved."***

7. If you are willing to trust Christ as your Saviour, please pray with me the following prayer:

Heavenly Father, I realize that I am a sinner. For Jesus Christ sake, please forgive me of my sins. I now believe with all of my heart that Jesus Christ died, was buried, and rose for me. Lord Jesus, please come into my heart and save my soul and change my life. Amen.

If you have any further questions regarding your salvation, please feel free to e-mail us at info@torchlegacy.com or you may call us at 1-877-TORCHLP.